The Pre-Med Bible
Effective Strategies and Practical Tips for Success with Medical School Admissions

Adam E. M. Eltorai

For my family

"No greater opportunity, responsibility, or obligation can fall to the lot of a human being than to become a physician. In the care of the suffering, he needs technical skill, scientific knowledge, and human understanding. He who uses these with courage, with humility, and with wisdom will provide a unique service for his fellow man and will build an enduring edifice of character within himself. The physician should ask of his destiny no more than this, he should be content with no less."

—*Harrison's Principles of Internal Medicine*

Contents

Introduction 11
Disclaimer 13

GPA and Courses
    Choose the Right Major 17
    Identify Your Target GPA and MCAT Score 19
    Course Requirements 21
    Map Out Your Four-Year Course Plan 23
    Take GPA Boosters 26
    Excel Your GPA 30
    Take as Many Classes as Necessary to Hit Your Target GPA 33
    Beat "Tough" Courses Elsewhere 36

Studying
    Ask Directly 43
    Flash Cards 45
    Do All the Problems 47
    Schedule Short Study Breaks 49
    Have Graders Proof Essays 51
    Plan Your Fun 52
    Eat well, Sleep Enough, Exercise Regularly 54

Extracurricular Activities
    Experience Most of the AMCAS Activity Categories 57

Do Activities that Yield Letters of Recommendation 61
Do Clinical Research 64
Start Doing Research Early 68
Get Published 70
Do Something Unusual Well 74
Be a Founder—Start Something 76
Commitment to Service 78
International Experience 80
Physician Shadowing 82

MCAT
Understand the MCAT 87
Master the MCAT 90

Applications
Understand the AMCAS Application 97
Letters of Recommendation 100
Personal Statement 104
Apply Early 106
Apply to Many Schools 108
Work on Secondary Applications before You Get Them 110
Make an Excel File for Application Materials 113

Interviews
Understand the Interview 117
Mock Interviews 120
List of FAQs on Interview Day 122

How to Answer the Two Big Interview Questions 126
Memorize Interview Answers 128
List of Questions to Ask on Interview Day 130
Scheduling Interviews 132
"In the Area" Preinterview E-mails 134
Multiple Mini-Interviews 135
Interview-Day Attire 137
Stay with a Student Host before Your Interview 139

After the Interview
Thank-You Notes 143
Update Letters of Interest 146
Letter of Intent 148
The Wait List 150
Ask Current Students How to Get Off the Wait List 153
Wait List Lobbyists 154
Stop Being Pre-Med 156

Additional Resources 157
Acknowledgments 158
About the Author 159

Introduction

Looking good on paper is the key to getting into medical school. The specific, up-to-date set of activities you need to do to look good on paper can be viewed as a checklist. How to complete the checklist most effectively is the subject of this book.

Much of the current advice on medical school admissions is outdated and/or is speculative. By removing the guesswork and uncertainty, you can be more confident that your efforts will pay off. Understanding what medical school admissions committees are looking for can help you plan and craft the profile of a strong applicant.

As someone who just completed the application process and was accepted by several of the most selective medical schools in the country, I am able to provide straightforward advice and practical tips based on tried-and-true experience.

First, read the book in its entirety, and then come back to it and use it as a reference. Use this book as a step-by-step guide, a recipe for success. The challenge of getting into medical school should be viewed as a game. I hope that this book will help make the "Pre-Med Game" easier and more enjoyable to play.

Disclaimer

Even after following the recommendations of this book, admissions to specific medical schools cannot be guaranteed. These pages contain information that has been personally useful. Medical school admissions committees have varying procedures and policies, which are subject to change. For the most up-to-date information about admissions at a particular medical school, please contact the school directly.

GPA and Courses

Choose the Right Major

Your GPA matters. The higher it is the better. Therefore, choose a major with courses that you will do well in. You will likely perform better if you are interested in the subject. Because you are only in college once, take advantage of the opportunity and study what excites you and will motivate you to excel.

You don't need to double major or major in a subject that is difficult for you because you think it will impress medical school admissions. Choose a major that makes your life easier and more enjoyable.

Regardless of the major you choose, you will have to complete the required medical school admission courses.

Minors also do not really matter. In other words, if it will cause you extra stress and/or hurt your GPA to tack on a minor in physics, don't do it. Your area of study is secondary to your GPA.

This philosophy also holds true for individual courses. Do not take non-required courses in which you will not get an A simply because you think it will be impressive to medical schools. Getting a C+ in Physical Chemistry is not impressive; it only hurts your GPA.

Identify Your Target GPA and MCAT Score

As soon as you know you are going to apply to medical school, purchase the latest edition of a book entitled *Medical School Admissions Requirements* (MSAR). Produced by the Association of American Medical Colleges (AAMC), the MSAR can be purchased at www.aamc.org/msar. The MSAR will be an invaluable resource. Familiarize yourself with all the specific schools you could ever imagine yourself applying to. Pay particular attention to each school's required course work and to the accepted students' average GPAs and MCAT scores.

With this knowledge you will know what courses you have to take in order to apply to particular schools (i.e., some schools have different requirements). By arming yourself with this information early, you will know what sort of GPA and MCAT score you will need to achieve in order to be competitive at a certain school.

Figure out the average GPA and MCAT scores of recently accepted applicants at your dream medical school. Make those your target numbers.

Course Requirements

Here is a list of the typical pre-med requirements:

- Biology: two semesters with lab; some schools also required additional advanced coursework in biology—the specific requirements vary from medical school to medical school.

- General Chemistry: two semesters with lab.

- Organic Chemistry: two semesters with lab.

- Physics: two semesters with lab.

- Math: two semesters of college math; some schools require specific courses (e.g., calculus or statistics).

- English: two semesters—at least one of which needs to be composition or a writing-intensive course.

Requirements for entry into a specific program vary. It is, therefore, essential to consult the MSAR when you first start planning your course schedule. Medical schools frequently do not accept AP course credit or course work taken abroad—particularly for required courses. Some requirements do not need to be completed before you apply, just prior to matriculation.

For school-specific questions, you can also contact the admissions offices directly or check out the schools' websites.

Map Out Your Four-Year Course Plan

Like most college students, you have eight semesters and three summers to complete your coursework. In addition to your college and major requirements, pre-medical students have the additional burden of completing medical school admissions requirements. With so many requirements, precise planning in advance is necessary.

As soon as you declare a major, map out your four-year course plan with exactly which courses you will take each semester and summer. Planning ahead will help you avoid scheduling conflicts and ensure that the courses you hope to take will be offered the semester you hope to take them.

Here are some things to keep in mind when planning your four-year course schedule:

- Take a light course load your freshman year. Give yourself the opportunity to transition into college. The increased demands and expectations of college courses, particularly in the sciences, can be a bit shocking at first. Start slowly; learn how to study at the college level, and then move into a more demanding schedule. Take only two science and/or math courses per semester your first year.
- Space out your heavy courses. You do not want to have a semester overloaded with too many time-consuming courses.
- After you map out when you will take the required and most demanding courses, fill the rest of your schedule with GPA-boosting classes and electives of interest.

- Some courses have prerequisites and, therefore, need to be taken in a particular sequence.
- Sign up for more classes than you will take in a semester. At the beginning of the semester, shop around for the classes—choosing the ones that seem easiest, most interesting, and fit best into your schedule. Drop the classes that you will not take.
- For familiarity with the MCAT material, complete the required pre-med courses before taking the MCAT.
- Do not take required courses pass/fail.
- Do not take required pre-med courses during a study abroad, as (most) medical schools will not accept such course credits.

In some cases, the required courses may not need to be completed before you submit your application, only before matriculation. Verify with individual medical schools' admissions offices.

Take GPA Boosters

Your GPA matters. Medical schools look at your overall GPA and your science GPA. Your overall GPA factors in your grades from every college course you have ever taken. Your science GPA factors in your grades from all biology, chemistry, physics, and math (BCPM) courses. The higher the two GPAs, the better.

Admissions officers look at many applications. They probably do not have the time to look at every college course each applicant has ever taken. When admissions officers get to the transcript portion of your application, they likely ask themselves the following questions about the applicant: *Did he or she complete all of the prerequisites? Does this applicant go to a reputable college? What are his or her overall and science GPAs? Are there any major red-flag grades on the transcript?*

Following that logic, the individual courses you take are of little importance to the admissions officer. If you got a C+ in your first semester of college, don't dwell on it. Move forward. Focus on taking courses that will help boost your GPA.

When planning your course schedule, be sure to investigate how easy it is to get an A in the class. To do this, you can 1) ask students you know who took the class how easy it is to get an A in this class; 2) look at previous years' student evaluations of the course and of the professor. These evaluations may be provided as a service through your college. If not, you can try the website www.ratemyprofessors.com.

An important note to be made is that on your AMCAS application, you are the one to designate the

BCPM courses that affect your science GPA. Obviously, most of the courses listed in the departments of biology, chemistry, physics, and math will factor into your science GPA.

However, there are courses in other departments that contain enough biology, chemistry, physics, or math to be classified as a BCPM course. Ask your pre-med advisor for this list. Incorporate courses from this list into your four-year course plan. If your advisor does not have such a list, take courses with titles that can reasonably be considered a BCPM course.

These courses can be a great source of science GPA boosting. Examples of such courses could be a neuroscience course listed in the Psychology Department that can be classified as biology; a biological anthropology course in the Anthropology Department can be classified as biology; an environmental science course could be classified as a physics or chemistry course; or a math course that is not offered by the Math Department. Courses that are interdisciplinary in nature are subject to your classification.

When it comes time to decide how to classify your courses on your AMCAS application, use your discretion reasonably and to the advantage of your GPA.

Excel Your GPA

Using the MSAR, identify past accepted students' average science and overall GPAs at all the schools you could ever imagine yourself applying to. Admissions committees like these GPAs and are, therefore, what you should aim to achieve. Although the higher the GPA, the better, you can still get an interview at a school if your GPA is a bit lower than the one reported in MSAR. Ideally, you want your GPA to be close, not more than 0.05 points below the one listed in MSAR.

Create a Microsoft Office Excel file for your GPA. In column one, put the names of your courses. In column two, put the number of credits/units/hours the course is worth. In column three, put the numeric value for the grade: A = 4.0, A− = 3.7, B+ = 3.3, B = 3.0, etc. Column four should be the product of columns two and three. For your GPA, divide the sum of column four by the sum of column two.

With this Excel file you will be able to figure out what grades you need to earn in how many units/credits/hours you need to hit your target GPA. *Do I have to get As in five units to get my GPA up to the desired 3.82? Or do I only have to get an A− in two units?* These questions frequently come up when planning your next semester's schedule and when you are finishing up a semester and trying to figure out how to allocate your limited study time for final exams.

This method can tell you whether you will be ready to apply at a certain time or whether you will need to take an extra semester of GPA-boosters to get your GPA where it needs to be.

Follow the same format to make an Excel file for your science GPA. As a reminder, your science GPA is made up of all the courses that are officially listed as and the ones that can reasonably be justified as being biology, chemistry, physics, and math.

Take as Many Classes as Necessary to Hit Your Target GPA

Your GPA matters, not the number of courses you have taken. If either or both your science and overall GPAs are significantly below your target numbers (see the "Identify Your Target GPA and MCAT Score" chapter), take more classes to increase your GPA. Calculate how many courses you will need to get As in to get your GPA to where it needs to be. Use the Excel file you created in the "Excel Your GPA" chapter to perform this calculation.

By mapping out your courses ahead of time, you can see where in your schedule you are able to take additional courses. Remember to maximize your summers. If taking additional courses during the semester will be too much and compromise your ability to get As in your other courses, you may consider delaying your application to take more courses. Taking an extra year to make sure your application is in order will not be frowned upon by medical school admissions—the admissions committee will really only look at your net result, your GPA.

If you decide to take extra time to boost your GPA, continue taking college courses rather than enrolling in a graduate program. If you take courses after your college graduation, consider taking courses at an easier place to increase the likelihood of getting all As (see the "Beat 'Tough' Courses Elsewhere" chapter). Do not enroll in a master's program. Graduate school classes do not factor into your college GPA—the GPA that medical school admissions officials care about.

If you have not completed the admission requirements, post-baccalaureate programs may be worth considering. These programs provide structure for college graduates to take additional college courses. Look into the details of the post-baccalaureate programs' requirements, advantages, and competitiveness. Consult with your pre-med advisor as to whether such a program is right for you.

Beat "Tough" Courses Elsewhere

Does a third of the organic chemistry class fail each year at your school? Or are you very uncomfortable with physics? If it is unlikely that you can get an A in a required course, there are several options worth considering:

- *Night school*: Many universities offer extension courses during the evening. Frequently, these courses are intended for people who work during the day and are going back to school. These types of students tend to be a bit older and several years out of school. Consequently, a night course's content may be less intense than the same course offered during the day. If you don't want to take general chemistry with all the pre-med, chemistry-major gunners, then consider this likely less competitive alternative to increase your chances of getting an A. It will not be apparent on your AMCAS application whether the course was taken in the night or day school—medical schools will only see that you took the course at your college.

- *Summer school*: Staying at your school over the summer to take tough courses offers several advantages. Frequently, summer-school courses are easier than their academic-year counterparts. Summer school is a great way to get a dreaded requirement out of the way relatively quickly, as opposed to struggling with the subject for an entire year. A course taken at your school over the summer will appear on your school's transcript and can count toward satisfying your college's graduation requirements. If the subject you choose to take is a challenging one for you, you will be able to focus your efforts on it more than during the year, when you are taking three to five other courses concurrently.

- *Easier school*: If your school is particularly challenging in one subject, look for alternative universities for summer school. Take that particularly challenging course at a school with a reputation for handing out more As. Ask people you know who have taken the course there how difficult the class was. Contact the potential course instructor and ask about his or her grading philosophy. Check out the website www.ratemyprofessor.com for student reviews of the course instructor. You do not need to get credit for a course at your college to use it for professional school admissions. If you need the credit for graduation, be sure to get the course approved by the appropriate people beforehand. *Notes*: Community college courses frequently do not satisfy medical school admissions requirements. Do not take all of your admissions requirements at an easier school, as it may appear you are deliberately avoiding challenging courses. Also, do not split sequential courses between institutions.

Remember that your GPA is what matters. Shop around for best place to get the A you need.

Studying

Ask Directly

If you have a question, ask the right person directly. Although this may seem obvious, sometimes people are afraid to ask. If you ask directly, you won't waste time worrying if the information you have is, in fact, accurate. Get the correct answer and move forward. Don't be afraid to be efficient. To put this advice into more concrete terms, here are a couple of illustrative examples:

- At the beginning of the semester, go to the professor's office hours and ask what you need to do to get an A+ in the course, how to best prepare for exams, and from what sources he or she draws test questions.

- If you have a question that is specific to a particular medical school, e-mail or call that admissions office directly.
- If you are considering taking a particular course, ask all your colleagues whether the course is good and/or easy. If you decide to take the class, ask everyone you know who took the class for their old exams. The more people you ask, the more likely you will get what you are looking for quickly.
- If you want to do something, ask the person in charge or his or her boss. Say, for example, you are interested in doing a summer internship at a biotech company. Interact with those who are in positions to give you what you want—contact the company president, CEO, or directors directly. With some searching and asking around, you should be able to find the relevant contact information.

Flash Cards

Arguably the best way to memorize anything is with flash cards. Because so many pre-med classes require significant memorization, how to use flash cards most effectively is worth discussing.

Go to class. Within several hours following a lecture, fill in any gaps in your notes, using your textbook or by contacting the instructor. Then rewrite all your now complete and accurate notes onto flash cards.

Starting two weeks before a test, begin reviewing the flash cards. As you go through the cards, make two piles: 1) "I know that material completely" and 2) "I need to keep reviewing that card." Go through the cards until all flash cards are in the first pile.

An implication of this study strategy is that you don't have to do all your textbook reading. Professors will lecture you on what they think is important and, therefore, what will be on the test. Master the lecture material and whatever else the professors explicitly say will be on the test. But do not waste your limited time doing extra reading. Presumably, if the textbook material were important, the professor would have mentioned it in class.

Do All the Problems

In classes that require problem solving on the tests (math, physics, chemistry), do all the problems you have on the subject material.

Professors may assign the odd-numbered problems for homework. In addition to the odd-numbered problems, do the even-numbered problems. Frequently, textbook problems are subtly different so as to test your thorough understanding of a subject. In order to differentiate students in the larger, introductory, "weed-out" classes, professors frequently like to test the subtleties of the material. Go into the test confident from solid preparation.

Even if you don't understand something, you will at least be familiar with it. If you tackle the problems early enough, you can ask the professor or TA to help you understand. It is vital to start studying at least two weeks before an exam in order to give yourself ample time to clear up any uncertainties you have about the material. If you still don't understand and the test is fast approaching, memorize how to solve the problem.

Redo old exams. Frequently, professors will recycle material. You may see the same questions reused, possibly with only slight modifications on test day. When going over the practice tests, understand why you got the questions you did wrong.

If practice or old tests are not handed out in class, ask everyone you know who took the class previously for them.

Schedule Short Study Breaks

Arguably, the hardest part of studying is simply getting started. To overcome this initial motivational barrier, start easy. Tell yourself, "In thirty minutes, I will take a break." Set a timer and get started. Take a five-minute break—use the timer to keep track. Study again for fifty minutes; take a five-minute break. Rinse and repeat. Before you know it, you will be moving through your studies. The timer puts pressure on you to keep going, but it also reminds you that a break is in the near future.

In order to keep breaks structured and short, it is essential that you do not have too many distractions. To avoid distractions, do not study in your room, and do not study in a group; find the place where you are most efficient (where there is the appropriate level of light, background noise, and movement)—go there, get your work done, then get out.

E-mailing and Facebooking are not the same as studying. Don't let these relatively mindless activities cut into the limited time you are awake and energized enough to focus on studying. Do avoid the distracting urge to check your e-mail. Try designating a typically unproductive but limited time each day to clearing out your inbox.

Have Graders Proof Essays

Write your papers early enough so that whoever is grading your paper (e.g., a TA or professor) can review and critique its weaknesses before it is due. Be sure to seek out the critique from the exact person who will be grading your paper. Fix the paper according to his or her suggestions. Giving the grader what he or she wants to see will increase your chances of earning a better grade.

Plan Your Fun

For sustained productivity, you must maintain balance in your life. In college and in work, balance is achieved by 1) doing something you enjoy, 2) prioritizing effectively, and 3) taking time for yourself.

Regardless of how busy you become, taking time for yourself is important. In order to make the most of this time, plan ahead. Whether it is going to a big party, watching a TV show, or simply hanging out with friends, scheduling your free-fun time beforehand will give you something to look forward to and motivate you to complete your less fun tasks. Additionally, you will enjoy your free time more, knowing that you are staying on schedule and not falling behind with your work.

A consequence of this approach is that it forces you to reduce unproductive or minimally beneficial time. In other words, avoid wasting time by being more efficient. Two simple steps you can implement to increase efficiency are 1) do not take breaks between classes, and 2) do not take prolonged lunches.

Eat Well, Sleep Enough, Exercise Regularly

Respect your body's needs. This part of life is basic but important. Doing these essential things will lead to increased efficiency and performance—making the rest of your life more enjoyable.

Extracurricular Activities

Experience Most of the AMCAS Activity Categories

On the AMCAS application, you categorize and write a brief description about each of the activities you were involved in. You may list up to fifteen experiences. The possible activity categories are paid employment (not military), paid employment (military), community service/volunteer (not medical/clinical), community service/volunteer (medical/clinical), research/lab, teaching/tutoring, honors/awards/recognitions, conferences attended, presentations/posters, publications, extracurricular/ hobbies/avocations, leadership (not listed elsewhere), intercollegiate athletics, artistic endeavors, and other.

If you "pass" your interview, you are considered a qualified applicant. Presumably then your name, GPA, MCAT score, undergraduate school, demographics, and whether or not you have experience in each of the activity categories is inputted into an Excel file along with all of the other admissible applicants. Emulating previous years' class compositions, the admissions committee likely goes through this file and chooses the applicants with particular characteristics that will yield a class with a desired composition.

To increase the chances of the admissions committee accepting you, do at least one activity in most of the experience categories. When picking activities to join, you can use your discretion as to whether the activities falls into a certain category. If you have completed an activity in most of the categories, when the admission committee is sorting the Excel file for an applicant that, for example, has experience in both artistic endeavors and clinical volunteering, your name will appear.

Thus, to ensure that your name satisfies all combinations of search criteria, aim to complete activities in each category. Although depth of experience is valuable, you do not want to have only seven different tutoring experiences listed on your application, as you will appear relatively one-dimensional. Breadth of experience is important when it comes to getting the initial interview offer and when the admissions committee is putting together the class and accepting applicants with certain compositions.

It is up to you how you classify your activities' category type on the AMCAS application. In other words, say you volunteered at a children's hospital teaching sick kids, for example. You also volunteered at a nursing home. Categorize the former activity as "teaching/tutoring" and the latter as "community service/volunteer (medical/clinical)." If you have participated in multiple smaller activities of the same category, you can group them into one of your fifteen AMCAS experiences. Wise categorization of activities will help you appear as a stronger candidate with a broader range of experiences.

When considering how you allocate your time, remember that your GPA and MCAT score are more important than your extracurricular experiences. Make sure that getting As in your coursework and scoring high on the MCAT remain a priority. Many extracurricular activities on an application cannot make up for a low GPA or MCAT score.

Do Activities That Yield Letters of Recommendation

To get strong letters, your letter writers should know you well. Letter writers will get to know you through significant interaction. The longer the association between you and your letter writer, the stronger the letter will probably be. It is helpful to identify potential letter writers early and work on developing those relationships.

For example, if you are participating in two extracurricular activities and only one has a faculty mentor (or someone in a meaningful position to write you a recommendation), focus more of your time where you are able to get a letter of recommendation.

If you are taking a class with a personable professor, attend his or her help-sessions and office hours, introduce yourself, and build a rapport. Take another one of course with the professor and get involved in something he or she does outside of lecture, like research or outreach. Joining a professor's research lab is a great way for him or her to get to know you. The more you do with the professor, the more he or she will get to know you, and the more things he or she will be able to discuss in your letter.

If you are already participating in an extracurricular, get to know someone in the organization whose letter would carry some weight (i.e., the person with an impressive title). Take on extra responsibilities or projects if it will increase your face time with this person. Seek his or her mentorship. Interacting with a mentor in multiple capacities will help the person to be able to craft a stronger letter, as he or she will be able to substantiate the letter with a greater number of concrete experiences. If you volunteer for a significant amount of time with a clinically-oriented program, physicians or other clinicians associated with the program could write meaningful letters.

For more information on letters of recommendation, see the chapter entitled, "Letters of Recommendation."

Do Clinical Research

Significant research is an unofficial requirement for medical school. Research is conducted in all academic disciplines, from anthropology, biology, comparative literature, and economics to psychology, chemistry, and physics. When deciding on the type of research to get involved in, you have many choices. In this chapter, an argument for getting involved in clinical research is presented.

The most straightforward way to get involved in clinical research is to e-mail physicians in fields of interest at the local medical school. Physicians were once pre-medical students themselves and, therefore, understand and appreciate what you are hoping to achieve through your research experience.

Look for the professors who have a strong track record of publication. To do so, search their names in PubMed (www.ncbi.nlm.nih.gov/pubmed/) to see if they have had several publications per year in the past several years. In your initial inquiry e-mail, express your interest in learning about their field before medical school. Ask if you can set up a brief meeting to chat about potentially joining their research team.

By e-mailing many academic physicians, you will likely only receive a response from several. Set up introductory meetings with the different physicians to meet each other and learn about the type of projects you could potentially work on. After meeting with several physicians, choose the one you are most interested in working with. Thank the other physicians you met with for their time, and inform them that you decided to work with another professor. Send a confirmation e-mail to the physician of choice and discuss starting logistics.

When you begin your research experience, remember your goal is to publish. To increase the likelihood of publication, focus on projects that will be completed in the shortest amount of time. If possible, get involved in nearly complete projects. Take the lead on your own simple project. If you take the lead on something, you won't have to depend on someone else to complete the project, and it will demonstrate initiative to your mentor.

Through a clinical research experience, you will interact with doctors and gain insight into a particular field of medicine. Your research mentor will likely be happy to discuss his or her experiences and offer advice on getting into medical school. If your mentor sees patients, you will have an easily accessible shadowing opportunity. When the time comes and you ask your physician mentor for a letter of recommendation, a strong letter from a physician will carry significant weight.

At your interviews, you will likely be interviewed by physicians. If you have researched something with clinical application, you will have something that is easy to discuss. Your clinical research may be more accessible than, say, a very esoteric basic science research project, and therefore, may be of greater interest to your interviewer. If you are able to discuss your research intelligently, you will come away looking like a well-informed applicant who has had relevant and useful clinical experience.

Start Doing Research Early

Start doing research as early as possible. The earlier you start, the higher the chances you will get published. Involvement in research is impressive. On paper, research experience demonstrates that you are academically driven and appreciate being intellectually challenged. By immersing yourself in a research project, you will feel as if you are a part of something bigger, which consequently may make your coursework seem a bit less daunting. By working with a professor for a significant amount of time, you will acquire a mentor who is more likely able to write you a strong letter of recommendation.

Research occurs in all disciplines at all colleges and universities to varying degrees. By the end of your freshman year, you may have an inkling as to fields of interest. Peruse the websites of the different departments of interest to get a sense of professors' research interests and projects. Contact professors of interest directly to set up meetings to discuss potentially joining their research team and what you would be working on. (For more on getting involved in research and how to choose a research mentor, see the "Do Clinical Research" chapter.)

An additional advantage to getting started with research early is that you can always switch research groups and work with different professors. If you find a particular lab or group to be unprolific with publications or unpleasant to work with, look for another research experience. Doing research in several different groups will appear on your application as having a breadth of interests.

Get Published

In academics, publications are the currency. Your application to medical school will be reviewed by academicians who value this currency. Generally speaking, other than letters of recommendation, publications are the only tangible things that can come from doing research. As an author on a publication, you will stand out from most other applicants who are likely unpublished. This chapter covers several tips for increasing the likelihood that you will have publications on your application.

Be the first-author on a publication. Taking the lead on a paper will give you greater control in the publication process. This will also demonstrate significant initiative and academic drive to medical school admissions committees and give your recommendation letter writers something tangible to tout. There are several strategies for accomplishing this.

- If you have done meaningful research for a course or a thesis, you could turn it into a publication. Express your interest in publishing your work to your instructors or research mentors. Ask them if they would be willing to help prepare the manuscript for publication. If an instructor helps you with editing and formatting of the paper, include him or her as a second author.
- If you work in a lab, ask your professor if he or she has a small publishable project that you could take the lead on.
- Write a review article or an editorial. Ask a professor if he or she would be willing to

review, edit, and revise it in return for co-authorship credit.
- If you are in charge of submitting the paper, pick a journal in which your paper is more likely to be accepted for publication. After a paper has been submitted to a journal for publication consideration, the review process can take several months. Thus, the journal where the paper is sent can determine whether or not you will have a publication on your application. For increased likelihood of your paper being accepted for publication, consider submitting your paper to a lower impact factor journal or an open-access journal. Find such journals with a quick Google search.

Another way to get publications is to publish abstracts. If you have data from an ongoing research experience, consider submitting an abstract (a short summary) of your work to a conference. It is acceptable to publish multiple abstracts on the same work by going to multiple conferences. If your abstract is accepted, you may be asked to present a poster of your work or give a short talk. These presentations will also enhance your application. If you are working with a professor, be sure to consult with him or her beforehand, get approval, and ask for recommended conferences to attend. With a quick search, you will probably be able to find local, regional, national, and international conferences throughout the year in many academic disciplines. There are also conferences geared toward undergraduates. These conferences can be a great way to ensure your abstract is accepted.

Do Something Unusual Well

Everyone is good at something. As long as it something you would feel comfortable discussing at an interview, it does not matter what the talent is. Whether you are a carp fishing tournament champion, professional harpist, iPhone app programmer, or have your own belly-dancing workout video, hone your unique skill and show it off. *Who wouldn't invite a champion unicyclist to interview?* Medical schools like to advertise that they have students accomplished in a diverse array of endeavors.

The admissions committee wants to see that you have outside interests, an indication that you are a normal and balanced person. You will stand out positively to admissions if you are able to demonstrate a tangible product or outcome from your unusual talent. This can be a great way to satisfy the "Extracurricular/hobbies/avocations" category of the AMCAS application.

Be a Founder—Start Something

A great way to be a standout medical school applicant is to be a founder. Start a charitable organization, a club, a website, a company, or a chapter of an established organization.

A practical way to become a founder, president, and/or CEO is to piggyback off an existing organization. For example, if you have been working with a campus community service organization for a while and you recognize an outstanding unmet need, branch off and create your own organization that satisfies that need. Your experience and connections with the existing organization will provide you with useful insights and resources as you develop your own organization. When it comes time to fill out your AMCAS application, you are a founder of a charitable organization—impressive!

Have you seen a club at another school that your school doesn't have? Contact the other school's club president and copy what the club is doing. For a health care economics class, did you have to propose a business solution to a public health problem? If so, run with the idea—work with the professor and create a startup company.

Commitment to Service

Pick any service-oriented activity and stick with it throughout college. On paper, this long-term experience demonstrates a commitment to service, something admissions wants to see on an application.

When picking such an activity, look for something meaningful that you would enjoy doing. Do something in which you are active and working toward a tangible goal, maybe with some sort of end product. If this volunteer activity is clinically-oriented, it could help inform your career interests. Because your time is valuable, look for something that is logistically convenient. Your college campus community service office is a great place to start your search for possible volunteer activities. Join an ongoing project in the local ER, serve meals at a soup kitchen, volunteer as a peer counselor, or be a Big Brother/Sister.

Such a long-term involvement could lead to a strong letter of recommendation and inspiring anecdotes for your personal statement and secondary application essays.

International Experience

Spending time in a different country and culture can offer you a new perspective and be an enriching experience. It is not uncommon for medical school applicants to have international experience(s) through international service trips or by studying abroad. If an international experience is something you are interested in and capable of doing, strongly consider the former option if you don't want to have to worry about grades while exploring different cultures.

There are frequently international service trips offered by different groups on college campuses. These trips often take place during school breaks. They are a nice way to do something productive and/or charitable while seeing new parts of the world. It is also a great way to make new friends. Given the typical short nature of these trips, you could potentially do multiple different trips to different places. If you wanted to demonstrate your leadership skills, you could team up with an established charitable organization and organize your own trip.

Many students opt to spend a semester studying abroad. Dependent on the program you go with, this could be the highlight of your college career. Studying abroad can be a great way to improve your foreign language skills. It is worth noting that the grades you earn abroad are viewed differently by different medical schools. Most medical schools will not accept pre-med requirements taken abroad. You will need to check with each school separately.

Physician Shadowing

Passively watching someone else work is not an accomplishment. The AMCAS application does not have a shadowing/clinical experience category. And you should not waste one of your recommendation letters on someone who can only attest to your "good watching skills." In other words, don't spend too much time shadowing. That said, however, some shadowing is expected, as it indicates that you are not making an uninformed decision about your career direction and have explored what patient care is like.

Concrete reasons for shadowing are the following:

- It can provide useful anecdotes for your personal statement.
- It can add a clinical flavor to a recommendation letter; you can ask a shadowed physician if she could send a brief comment to one of your letter writers to quote.
- If you have extra space on your AMCAS application and have done a lot of shadowing, you may consider including "Physician Shadowing" as an "Other" activity.

Maximize your returns from shadowing by shadowing multiple physicians in different specialties only one time. On paper, shadowing a diverse array of specialties is more impressive than having observed one person for hundreds of hours, as it demonstrates you have exposure to a greater breadth of the many fields of medicine.

The simplest way to shadow a physician is to ask. Contact doctors of interest directly and say you are interested in learning about their field and inquire whether it would be possible to observe them as they see patients. Physicians at academic centers tend to be receptive to shadowing inquiries, given that they are affiliated with teaching hospitals.

When you shadow, get a sense of the specialty, its culture, the types of problems that are dealt with, and the physicians' personalities and outlook. While your shadowing experience is still fresh in your mind, jot down any meaningful experiences that you observed or lessons learned that you can potentially use in your personal statement or secondary application essays.

MCAT

Understand the MCAT

Along with your GPA, your Medical College Admissions Test (MCAT) score is the single most important component of your application. Medical school admissions committees care about your numbers—science GPA, overall GPA, and MCAT score—because they have predictive value. A high GPA indicates that you are academically focused and will likely be capable of handling the rigors of medical school. A high MCAT score means that you are a good standardized test taker and will likely to perform well on the standardized medical licensing exams. High licensing exam scores increase a medical student's chances of competitive residency placement. The better the residency placement of a medical school's graduates, the better the school looks. Thus, medicals schools seek to admit students who are likely to make them look good down the road.

The MCAT consists of four sections: Verbal Reasoning (VR), Biological Sciences (BS), Physical Sciences (PS), and Writing (WR). The VR section tests critical thinking and reasoning skills. The BS section tests problem solving and knowledge of concepts in biology and organic chemistry. The PS section tests problem solving and knowledge of concepts in physics and general chemistry. These three sections are each scored on a scale of 1 (low) to 15 (high), for a composite score of up to 45. The WR section is based on two essays that are scored on a scale of J (low) to T (high). The composite score out of 45 is much more important than your WR score.

Take the exam when you know you will be well prepared. If you do not achieve your desired score, you can retake the exam. Medical schools see all of your scores, so multiple retakes is not recommended. Some students opt for a gap year so that they have additional time to study for and complete the MCAT successfully.

By knowing your MCAT score early, you can determine whether you are ready to apply. At the latest, have your MCAT scores available before you apply in June so that you can still apply to medical school as early as possible. For more information on the importance of applying early, read the "Apply Early" chapter. MCAT scores are usually available thirty days after taking the test. Medical schools consider only MCAT scores that are no more than three years old.

For information on how to prepare for the MCAT, read the "Master the MCAT" chapter.

Master the MCAT

Arguably, your MCAT and GPA are equally important when it comes to medical school admissions. You spend three to four years working on your GPA. Make sure to treat your MCAT preparation with the same level of commitment and dedication. Because proper MCAT preparation is time consuming and can be stressful, you should aim to take the test only once.

The MCAT is given multiple times a year. The test schedule can be found at: www.aamc.org/students/mcat/. Because most college courses are not designed specifically for the MCAT, it is important to study explicitly for the MCAT.

Ideally, here is how to prepare effectively for the MCAT: enroll in a formally structured, year-long MCAT review course (e.g., Kaplan, www.kaptest.com/mcat or The Princeton Review, www.princetonreview.com/mcat/) starting in the fall. Attend class and do all the homework. Then devote the entire following summer exclusively to daily, full-length practice tests. Take the real test toward the end of the summer.

When planning your class schedule, reduce your course load to compensate for the additional time commitment of the MCAT review course. During the school year, MCAT preparation should be treated as a three- to five-unit class. During the summer, the MCAT should be your major focus; involvement in any other activities is not recommended.

Make sure that the review course you choose to enroll in provides you with many computer-based, full-length practice tests that you are able to access throughout your entire preparation period. Doing practice tests on the computer will help to simulate real test-day conditions. Make sure to take practice tests where you are free from distractions—other people, phones, Internet, etc.

After spending the academic year in the review course, learning the exam structure and content, along with test-taking strategies, the summer should be devoted to practice tests. Your MCAT score will be a reflection of how well you know the test, not necessarily a reflection of your knowledge of particular subjects. Thus, do many practice tests to get better at performing well on the MCAT. By taking many practice tests, you will also build up your test-taking stamina.

At the beginning of the summer, take a full-length test every other day. Spend non-test days thoroughly reviewing only the problems you missed. Understand why you got the problems you missed wrong by reviewing the correct answers. If you are consistently missing the same type of questions, go back and review that subject's content. Other than those instances, do not spend significant time during the summer memorizing rarely tested content.

Make note of your practice test scores to monitor your progress. Individual test scores may vary greatly in the beginning. Your scores will become more predictable the more tests you take. As the summer progresses, begin taking daily full-length practice tests at the same time of the day you are scheduled to take your real test. You can be confident that you are ready when you are consistently scoring at or above your desired score. Continue to review why you got the questions you did wrong. As you approach test day, be sure to get adequate rest and proper nutrition.

Applications

Understand the AMCAS Application

The American Medical College Application Service (AMCAS) application is the common application you will submit to the designated US medical schools of your choosing the summer a year before you plan to start medical school. Understanding what the medical school admissions offices see can help you craft your ideal on-paper image. The AMCAS application includes the following:

- Identification information
- Contact information

- Biographic information
- Demographic information
- Family information
- Schools attended
- Transcript (For each college class you took, you list where you took the course, the course name and number, when you took it, the grade earned, the number of credit hours, and whether the course will factor into your science GPA or just your overall GPA.)
- GPA summary
- MCAT scores
- Experiences (You can list up to fifteen different experiences. There is room for a brief description of each experience. You are given additional descriptive space for the three experiences you consider to be most meaningful. You also categorize the activity type—see the "Experience Most of the AMCAS Activity Categories" chapter for more information.)

- Personal statement (See the "Personal Statement" chapter for more information.)
- Names of people the letters of recommendation will be coming from

You will need to request that official transcripts be forwarded to AMCAS from all the colleges you attended. Obtain a copy of each of your official transcripts yourself to use in completing the transcript section of your AMCAS application. AMCAS validates the accuracy of your reported grades before sending the application to the medical schools.

Letters of Recommendation

For your application, you will need to submit three to five letters of recommendation, with at least two coming from science faculty. You should submit letters from professionals who know your capabilities, personality, and quality of work. For more information on cultivating relationships that will lead to letters of recommendation, review the "Do Activities That Yield Letters of Recommendation" chapter.

If you are majoring in the sciences, get to know your advisor, take his or her class, and do well in the class. Note: With regard to letters from science faculty, some schools do not accept letters from research lab mentors in place of someone who has taught you in a classroom setting. Be sure to check individual schools' policies.

In planning your on-paper image, pick the types of letter writers you want to have supporting you *a priori*. In other words, if you want an artistic dimension to your application, take banjo lessons throughout college with the same music teacher. If you want to convey an interest in athletics, get a letter from a famous sports medicine cardiologist or orthopedic surgeon by joining his or her research team and by shadowing him or her.

Something to keep in mind when considering who to ask for a letter of recommendation: the recommender's professional title carries weight. The medical school admissions committee will consist of individuals who work in an academic setting, where titles are considered important. Receiving a supportive letter from a big-name professor or physician will help your application.

Be tactful when it comes to requesting letters of recommendation. Schedule an appointment to meet with your mentor to discuss your goals and plans. Your mentor will likely know that the purpose of the meeting is for you to ask for a letter of recommendation. The best way to phrase your request is as follows: "Would you be willing to write a letter in support of my medical school application?" Be sure to ask for your letter at least four weeks in advance of its due date in order to give your writer enough time to write it.

Bring to the meeting a packet for your letter writer. The packet should contain your current resume, unofficial transcripts, a preaddressed envelope, and instructions on how, where, and by when to submit the letter.

Only when the medical schools receive the letters of recommendation will they begin to review your entire application. Therefore, have your writers submit their letters early. Your letters are usually submitted to your school's pre-med office or directly to AMCAS. Check with your school's pre-med office for letter-submission specifics.

After the letter is submitted, handwrite a thank-you note to your recommenders. When you are accepted, write another thank-you note, updating them on where you will be going to medical school.

Personal Statement

The personal statement is the essay portion of the AMCAS application that explains your motivation and suitability for pursuing a career in medicine. The goal of the personal statement essay is to humbly sell yourself. To achieve this goal effectively, write a clear, logical narrative that discusses career-directing lessons you learned from several specific, meaningful experiences. The lessons you discuss should demonstrate how you have maturely gone through a process of careful reflection and self-examination.

Your personal statement can be up to 5,300 characters. Strong personal statements are interesting to read, insightful, and revealing. The tone should be straightforward, honest, and not self-congratulatory. A well-written personal statement could potentially mitigate a weaker writing score on the MCAT.

Because this is a task that requires careful planning, it is important to start working on the personal statement well in advance. Try writing the first draft the year before you apply. This will give you time to revisit and revise your essay several times. Take drafts to advisors, professors, research mentors, writing instructors, and physicians who will read them critically for you.

Apply Early

Each medical school has a set number of interview slots and class positions. By completing your application early, you will be considered for an interview when the greatest number of interview slots is open. Then, if you complete your interview early at a medical school that accepts applicants on a rolling basis, you will be considered for admission when the greatest number of class positions is open.

When you apply early, you will be compared to a relatively smaller pool of applicants, in which case you are more likely to appear to be a stronger applicant. In other words, as the application season progresses, the admissions committee will have seen a greater number of strong applicants who will raise the bar for what it takes to get an interview offer. The same applicant who gets an interview early in the application season may not be offered one later.

AMCAS must verify the accuracy of your submitted application (i.e., to see if the grades you listed correspond with the ones on your transcripts). The earlier you submit your AMCAS application, the shorter the verification time and the quicker your application is sent to the medical schools. During peak AMCAS submission periods, when many applications are flooding into the AMCAS system, the verification process can take several weeks.

In the past, applicants were able start working on their AMCAS applications beginning in May and were able to submit the applications beginning in June. Check with AMCAS directly for specifics of your application year.

Apply to Many Schools

To increase your chances of being accepted, apply to a lot of medical schools. Much like a raffle, the more tickets you have in play, the more likely you are to win.

It is difficult to predict where you might get accepted. There are few guarantees that one particular school will accept you. You may be surprised by rejections from "safety" schools and acceptances from "reach" schools. Do not be afraid to apply to medical schools that report accepting applicants with higher

GPAs and MCAT scores than your own. The reported average GPA and MCAT scores for accepted applicants may be slightly inflated compared to the actual class composition. The school may accept numerically-strong applicants who choose to matriculate elsewhere. This means that the school also admits applicants whose GPA and MCAT scores are lower than a school's reported scores.

Although applications are costly in money and time, they should be viewed as an investment. You will have already spent years and thousands of dollars preparing to apply. Don't skimp on the last step. Additionally, there are financial assistance programs that can ease the application costs (see "Additional Resources" for more information).

As with college applications, apply to "reach," "target," and "safety" schools. Apply to multiple schools in each category. Be sure also to apply to all your dream schools and all of your home state schools. It is not uncommon to apply to over thirty schools—cast a broad net.

Work on Secondary Applications before You Get Them

After medical schools receive your verified application from AMCAS, most will send you a secondary application. Secondary applications generally consist of additional questions in the form of short essays. Medical schools will not review your file and consider you for an interview until you have submitted your secondary application and your application is complete. Thus, it is important to complete your secondary applications as early as possible. (For an explanation on the importance of submitting your application early, see the "Apply Early" chapter.)

You can work on the secondary application essays before the medical schools send them to you. Each year, medical schools generally repeat their essay questions with slight modifications. Earlier years' questions are posted online on a website called Student Doctor Network (forums.studentdoctor.net/). You should be able to find each school's questions listed from the previous years.

By anticipating the essay questions and drafting your response, you will be able to submit your secondary applications sooner. Because the essay questions may change from one year to the next, make sure that you are answering the questions you are actually being asked. Frequently, the essay questions from different medical schools are quite similar. After you have written several secondary application essays, you may be able to recycle some of your responses.

A reasonably ambitious goal could be to submit secondary applications within twenty-four hours of receiving a request from a medical school. Doing this will prevent the accumulation of secondary applications in your e-mail inbox. Completing your application early will convey to an admissions committee that you are on top of things and interested in their school.

Make an Excel File for Application Materials

When you start receiving secondary applications, you will likely receive many within a short period of time. It is important to be systematic about completing the secondary applications quickly and effectively. A simple way to keep organized is to make a Microsoft Excel file for your application materials.

In this file, create column headers with the following titles: school name, date secondary requested, date secondary fee paid, date secondary submitted, date school confirmed receiving recommendation letters, application notes (login info and passwords), date of interview, and update letters submitted on [dates].

Update the Excel file as items are completed. Develop a system to indicate whether something needs to be completed immediately or if you are waiting for a medical school to confirm that an item has been received.

Interviews

Understand the Interview

The purpose of the interview is to see if you are "normal," to assess your interpersonal skills, and to get a better understanding of you and your motivation for applying to that specific program. Admissions committees seek students who are positive, genuine, thoughtful, logical, and capable of coherent conversation. Most interviews are twenty- to sixty-minute conversations. Interviewers are not out to get you or throw you curveballs. The most seasoned interviewers are able to put the interviewees at ease immediately. Frequently, the interviewers are older, semi-retired physicians. You may also be interviewed by current students, younger faculty, or other admissions officers.

It is important to prepare for your interview. Inquire about the interview a day before you go. *How many separate interviews will you have? Who will be interviewing you? What will each different interviewer assess you on? Will the interviewer be familiar with your application before you meet ("open file")? Does the school do one-on-one, group, panel, and/or multiple mini-interviews?* Gather this information by contacting current students at the school and the admissions office directly. If you do not know anybody at the specific school personally, you can ask the admissions office for contact information for student ambassadors.

Having a better understanding of what to expect, the types of questions, and any unusual things to be aware of before your interview day will alleviate any uncertainty. After a couple of interviews, you will start to feel more comfortable with the interview process.

The night before your interview, be sure you know exactly where you need to be the next day. Go and physically check out the interview site to ensure you don't get lost on interview day. Also, review your written-out answers to the frequently asked interview questions (see the "List of FAQs on Interview Day" chapter), review your AMCAS and secondary application materials, review unique features about the school, and make sure your clothes are ironed and ready.

Mock Interviews

Conduct mock interviews to help you feel a bit more comfortable going into your first couple of real medical school interviews. Initially, you can ask your friends and family to help you practice. But be sure not to practice only with them, as they know you and already think you are great. For a more useful mock interview experience, practice with someone you are not as familiar with. Frequently, college career centers offer mock interviews. Ask your professors and advisors and/or physicians you know if they will conduct practice interviews with you and give you feedback. Try wearing your actual interview-day attire in order to get used to answering interview questions in the formal outfit. For a list of questions to practice with, see the "List of FAQs on Interview Day" chapter.

The more mock interviews you do, the more confident you will become with your interviewing skills. Ask your practice interviewers for critical feedback. *Were my responses clear? How was my body language? What were my weaknesses?* Use that feedback to improve. Refine your responses; focus on clearly articulating your responses with brevity.

List of FAQs on Interview Day

To read questions that recent applicants were asked at specific schools, check out the Student Doctor Network interview threads. You may be asked some of the same questions at your upcoming interview. Go to studentdoctor.net/schools/. Click the name of the school you are interested in. Under "Interview Feedback," click "View survey results." On the next page, scroll down and click "Questions." Peruse the page that opens. Recent past interviewees have written down specific, interesting, and difficult questions they were asked on their interview day. Review these questions, think of how you would answer them. If you see a specific question that was asked of many applicants, there is a good chance you may be asked it, too. Also peruse this website for other information about the structure of the school's interview day and useful things to know beforehand.

Prepare and memorize clear and to-the-point answers to the commonly asked interview questions listed below. You might get several of these questions on your interview day:

- Tell me about yourself.
- Why do you want to be a doctor?
- Why are you interested in attending this medical school?
- What are you looking for in a medical school?
- How did you decide to go into medicine?
- What do you do for fun?
- What are your weaknesses?
- Tell me more about your [one of your experiences].
- What are the qualities of a good doctor?

- Who has been your most influential figure?
- Tell me about a particularly challenging time in your life or about a time you failed.
- Do you want to add anything that we didn't cover in this interview?
- What questions do you have for me?
- If you had to choose a career other than medicine, what would it be?
- What do you see yourself doing in twenty years?
- What do you think will be your greatest challenge in completing medical school?
- Tell me about your family.
- How do you achieve balance in your life?
- In your view, what is the most pressing problem facing medicine today?
- Which area of medicine interests you the most?
- What unique quality do you bring to the entering class?
- How did you choose your undergraduate school? How has your experience been?

- What have you been doing since your college graduation?

How to Answer the Two Big Interview Questions

Interviewers at many schools will ask you 1) Why medicine? 2) Why this school of medicine? Here are recommendations for how to answer these questions:

1) I am interested in the application of science to solve real problems and because I believe that caring for the sick in the capacity of a physician is a worthwhile pursuit.

2) When looking into which medical schools to apply to, I looked for schools that met three criteria:
    a. Schools that genuinely value medical student education; institutions that invest in their student growth and development.
    b. Schools with the resources—the caliber of students it attracts, the faculty, the facilities, the university, or the surrounding community—to offer a strong medical education.
    c. And schools that subjectively feel like the right fit.

Based on what I have learned about this school, it appears to fit the bill.

Memorize Interview Answers

Write out succinct answers to each question in the "List of FAQs on Interview Day" chapter. Your written responses should be clear and to the point. Memorize your responses. Rehearse your answers—practice saying them. Make sure they do not sound canned or mechanical by including natural pauses. Have your mock interviewers ask you some of the questions and give you feedback. If you prepare and memorize answers to all the FAQs, you can be confident in your ability to answer most interview questions. Even if you are asked a totally new question, you can draw on ideas and phrases you have memorized from answers to other questions.

Adjust and improve your responses. Rewrite them and rehearse saying the new version. Continual modification of your answers over time will lead to a polished interview performance.

Carry a copy of the answers to the FAQs in the black leather folder that you carry around with you on interview day. Frequently there is down time, and this can be a nice thing to review before you are called to interview.

During the real interview, the questions could be worded differently. Interviewers at different schools will ask a different set of the FAQs, depending on the typical type of applicant they interview. Take your time to listen and recognize which of the FAQs is being asked. Think about the response that you have practiced. Then respond clearly, calmly, and confidently.

List of Questions to Ask on Interview Day

On your interview day, you will be asked by your interviewers, the admissions officers, and current students if you have any questions. The following three questions will make you look good on interview day and are all you need to remember:

- Are there things you would change about the medical school?
    - This question is a tactful way to ask about a school's weaknesses. Such a

question demonstrates that you think critically.
- Can you speak to the level of accountability and responsibility of third and fourth year medical students?
    - This question demonstrates that you are interested in the quality of the clinical experience you could receive at the school.
- Can you speak to the level of faculty support medical students receive?

Scheduling Interviews

If you are offered an interview at a school that accepts students on a rolling basis, it is important to interview earlier rather than later in the season because there are more acceptance positions available earlier in the application season. If it a non-rolling admission school, your date of interview is not as important because all applicants are reviewed and chosen on one date.

If you are scheduling more than one interview at a certain time, schedule a school that is lower on your ranked list for an earlier date because it takes a couple of interviews to feel comfortable interviewing. It is better to do your more important interviews after you have had some practice and are more confident with your interviewing skills.

"In the Area" Preinterview E-mails

If you are going to be in the area near a school that has not offered you an interview (i.e., interviewing at a different medical school in the same city/region), it may not hurt to contact the admissions office of that school and say something along these lines: "I will be in the Boston area during the week of October 11. If you are considering offering me an interview, I would greatly appreciate it if you could let me know as soon as possible so that I may potentially consolidate my travels from California."

Multiple Mini-Interviews

Several medical schools have started using multiple mini-interviews (MMI). MMI consist of eight to ten different stations where you are asked to answer questions on various hypothetical and ethical questions. Because the questions do not have correct answers per se and are unpredictable, the best way to prepare is to understand how to structure your responses in a clear and thoughtful manner.

Most of the questions you will be asked will require you to consider two opposing views. Using an example, here is the basic format for answering many of the questions you might encounter in an MMI:

- This question appears to revolve around the balance between 1) the individual's right to privacy and 2) the importance of community safety.
- On one hand, the individual's right to privacy is supported by the following arguments...
- On the other hand, the importance of community safety is supported by the following arguments...
- After considering both sides, I believe that the arguments in favor of community safety outweigh the arguments for the individual's right to privacy for the following reasons...

Interview-Day Attire

You do not want to stand out because of your clothes. Your look should be conservative, neat, and professional. Gentlemen should wear a dark (navy blue or black) suit, white shirt, simple-patterned or solid-colored tie, black leather belt, black dress socks, and black shoes with laces that match the belt. Ladies should wear a dark (navy blue or black) knee-length skirt or pantsuit, light-colored blouse, and black, closed-toe shoes with not-so-high heels. Makeup and accessories should be simple and display professionalism.

Most applicants carry with them a black leather folder. Inside the folder, carry a copy of your AMCAS application, your secondary application, notes about the school, your answers to the frequently asked interview questions, a pen, and a notepad.

Stay With a Student Host before Your Interview

When scheduling your interview, you will usually be given the opportunity to stay with a student host the night before your interview. Staying with a student the night before offers many benefits. It is a great way to get to know the type of students at the school. The students are usually more than happy to talk about their interview-day experience and share any school-specific interview insights. They will frequently walk you to your interview in the morning, thus alleviating any unnecessary stress over directions in a new setting. During your interview itself, you can mention that you have been impressed with the caliber of students you have interacted with.

After your interview, your student host can help answer questions you may have. Be sure to thank your host. You can offer to buy your host dinner, give him or her a gift certificate, or simply write a thank-you note.

After the Interview

Thank-You Notes

Within a day following your interview, send thank-you notes to your interviewers. Thank the dean and director of admissions for the opportunity. If you interacted with other members of the admissions committee or staff during your interview day, you can also send them brief thank-you notes. It is better to thank too many people than too few. The notes can be handwritten or e-mailed. A handwritten note is a bit more special and, therefore, memorable. But if you are sending a thank you to a student interviewer, an e-mail may suffice. You want your notes to come off as sincere, so use your discretion with whom and how you thank them.

Frequently, at the end of your interview, your interviewers will give you their contact information. If not, you can ask them: "I would like to send you a proper thank-you note. How should I go about doing this?" Before you leave your interview day, ask the admissions staff more details about submitting thank-you notes. The content of your thank-you notes can generally along these lines:

Dear Dr. Smith,

Thank you for taking the time to interview me on November 4. I enjoyed meeting you and learning about Wadsberg School of Medicine. I believe that Wadsberg would be a great fit for me. I appreciate how the school values medical student education and supports a breadth of meaningful opportunities. I would be honored to join the Wadsberg community. Please let me know if there is anything else you need to evaluate my candidacy.

Sincerely,
Adam Eltorai
ae5674@yahoo.com

Update Letters of Interest

These letters express continued interest in attending a medical school. Many medical schools will accept these letters only after you have interviewed. These should include notable accomplishments that you believe will enhance your application (e.g., awards, publications, and/or other remarkable scholarly/extracurricular endeavors). These letters could also include why you remain interested in attending that particular school, why you believe it is a good fit, and possibly what you could bring to the entering class. After you have completed an interview at a certain school, you should submit these letters periodically to demonstrate continued interest in the school. You should date the letter, include the subject of the letter (RE: Update Letter), and address it to the Members of the Admissions Committee. The letters should be attached to e-mails as PDFs. Submit an average of one to two of these letters per month until you are accepted or rejected. Call the admissions office directly and ask about the optimal frequency and content of these letters.

If it is getting late into the interview season and you have yet to receive an offer to interview from a particular school, an update letter/letter of interest may be useful.

Letter of Intent

Medical schools like to be viewed as selective by keeping their acceptance rates down. One way they do this is by offering admission to the students who are most likely to matriculate. Consequently, an applicant can submit a letter to that effect. This letter includes the phrase "If you accept me, I will matriculate." Although not a legally binding document, only one of these letters should be submitted to your absolute top-choice school.

This letter is most useful to get off wait lists. You may not want to submit this letter too early, as where you want to go to school may actually change over the course of the application year. Contact the medical school admissions office directly and ask about submission of a letter of intent—how useful is the submission of such a letter, to whom it should be sent, optimal submission date, etc.

The Wait List

After you interview at a school, you will be accepted, rejected, or placed on the wait list. Applicants who are put on the wait list are considered admissible. For a medical school that has class sizes of one hundred students, the admissions committee initially offers admission to only one hundred applicants. When the admissions committee is first putting together the class, it probably goes through the list of admissible applicants and chooses applicants with particular characteristics that will yield a class with a desired composition, which is likely to be quite similar to previous years' class compositions.

By a particular day in late spring of the application year, after interviews are complete, applicants with multiple acceptance offers turn down all but one of the schools that accepted them. At this time, all applicants can hold their wait list positions. When an accepted applicant chooses to attend a different school or defers matriculation for the year, a position opens up in that school's entering class. The admissions committee will then refill the class to one hundred students by offering acceptance to wait-listed applicants.

Some schools rank their wait-listed applicants, while others don't. For schools that do rank their wait lists, admissions committees admit wait-listed applicants in their ranked order as class positions open up. Presumably, for the schools that do not rank their wait lists, wait-listed applicants are accepted based on having a GPA, MCAT score, undergraduate school, demographics, and/or categories of activities experienced to a student who turned down their acceptance.

Ask Current Students How to Get Off the Wait List

During your interview day, you will likely be given a list of student e-mail addresses you can contact if you have questions about the school. If you are wait-listed, contact these students and ask them to advise you on how to get off the wait list. These students may have been on the wait list themselves the previous year and can suggest practical steps to take to get accepted off the wait list.

Wait List Lobbyists

If you are wait-listed, it is important to continue to express interest in attending the school. If you have friends who are current students, ask them to advocate on your behalf to the admissions committee. If you know a faculty member or another individual with clout, ask him or her to advocate on your behalf. You can ask the people who initially sent in letters of recommendation to submit follow-up supportive e-mails or letters. Ask for letters of recommendation from new people who will strengthen your application. Ask your pre-med advisor to call the dean/director of admissions and lobby on your behalf. Tell your interviewer that you were wait-listed and remain interested in attending the school, and that you would appreciate it if they could help advocate on your behalf.

Don't be afraid to ask for help. If you have been wait-listed, the medical school already thinks you are a strong candidate. If the admissions office receives lots of letters and phone calls supporting your application, they will know that you are still interested in attending. Why else would you spend time and energy asking lobbyists for support?

Stop Being Pre-Med

Once you are accepted and know where you are going to medical school, take some time to breathe, recharge, and celebrate your accomplishment. You have made it through the bottleneck and won the "Pre-Med Game." Congratulations! You are in the system and are eventually going to be a doctor.

Additional Resources

Additional Application Services:

> Texas Medical and Dental Schools: www.utsystem.edu/tmdsas/
>
> Ontario Medical Schools: www.ouac.on.ca/omsas/
>
> American Association of Colleges of Osteopathic Medicine: aacomas.aacom.org/

AMCAS: www.aamc.org/amcas

> Financial Assistance Program: www.aamc.org/students/applying/fap/

MCAT: www.aamc.org/students/mcat/

Medical School Admissions Requirements (MSAR): www.aamc.org/msar

Student Doctor Network: www.studentdoctor.net

Acknowledgments

Special thanks to David Holtzman, MD; Paul Stein, PhD; B. Ruth Clark, PT, PhD; Robert Sussman, PhD; Amanda Kirkpatrick; Carolyn Herman; Joan Downey, MD, MPH; Gregory Polites, MD; John Morton, MD, MPH; Emily Guhl; and Oliver Jawitz. I offer an especially heartfelt thank you to my parents, J.P. and Mahmoud.

About the Author

Adam E. M. Eltorai graduated *summa cum laude* from Washington University in St. Louis. He received offers of admission with merit scholarships from multiple medical schools. He is currently a medical student at Brown University and lives in Providence, Rhode Island.

www.ingramcontent.com/pod-product-compliance
Lightning Source LLC
Chambersburg PA
CBHW071722090426
42738CB00009B/1846